HAUNTED PLACES

HAUNTED HOUSES & MANSIONS

by Janie Havemeyer

BrightPoint Press

San Diego, CA

BrightPoint Press

an imprint of ReferencePoint Press, Inc.
Printed in the United States

For more information, contact:
BrightPoint Press
PO Box 27779
San Diego, CA 92198
www.BrightPointPress.com

LIBRARY OF CONGRESS CATALOGING-IN-PUBLICATION DATA

Name: Havemeyer, Janie, author.
Title: Haunted houses & mansions / by Janie Havemeyer.
Description: San Diego, CA: ReferencePoint Press, 2026 | Series: Haunted places | Audience: Grade 7 to 9 | Includes bibliographical references and index.
Identifiers: ISBN: 9781678211844 (hardcover) | ISBN: 9781678211851 (eBook)
The complete Library of Congress record is available at www.loc.gov.

CONTENTS

AT A GLANCE

- Haunted houses and mansions are places that are believed to be occupied by ghosts.
- Houses and mansions that are believed to be haunted often have stories connected to them. These could be murders or deaths that have happened in them.
- There is no solid proof that ghosts are real. But many people still believe in them.
- Experts in ghost hunting are called paranormal investigators or ghost hunters. They gather evidence at supposedly haunted places.
- Paranormal investigators look for signs that a house might be haunted, including strange smells, unexplained noises or voices, or ghostly figures.

- The White House is one of the most famous haunted mansions in the United States. People often report seeing the ghost of President Abraham Lincoln there.
- Some other famous US houses and mansions that are believed to be haunted include the Amityville Horror House, the Winchester Mystery House, and the Lizzie Borden House.
- Many people travel across the United States to visit spooky homes. They take tours through them and even spend the night in hopes of capturing evidence of hauntings.

THE PERRON FARMHOUSE

The Perron family moved into a farmhouse in January 1971. It was located in Burrillville, Rhode Island. The house was built in 1736. Over the years, it had many owners. The Perrons were excited to buy a home with a long history.

One night, 7-year-old Cindy Perron lay in her bed. Her mother, Carolyn, had just tucked her in. After Carolyn left, a ghostly lady appeared. The figure leaned over to

The Perron farmhouse is also known as the Conjuring House.

GHOST
GHOST

kiss Cindy goodnight. The figure smelled like flowers and fruit. Cindy trembled in fear as the figure disappeared out her door.

The next day, Carolyn heard about Cindy's ghost. Carolyn asked her five daughters if they had also noticed strange things occurring in the house. Christine claimed that her toys moved around when

The spirit of a woman named Bathsheba is believed to haunt the Perron farmhouse.

Ghosts that can move objects are sometimes called poltergeists.

she left her room. Nancy said she heard loud footsteps in her closet. Her closet door would also open when no one was around.

Carolyn told her daughters she believed she had seen a ghost one morning by her bed. It was dressed in an old-fashioned green dress. She asked why no one had spoken up before. The girls thought they had been imagining things. But now, the Perrons wondered whether their house was haunted.

Some people think that hauntings are real, but others say there are scientific explanations for unexplained activity.

HOUSE AND MANSION HAUNTINGS

The Perron farmhouse is just one of many houses and mansions that are considered haunted. A haunted house or mansion is a place that is believed to be occupied by ghosts. People who live in these buildings report things that are not easily explained. These might include strange smells and noises. Some people even claim to see ghostly figures.

Haunted houses grab the attention of both ghost hunters and everyday people. People are curious about the unknown. Many people search for answers for unexplained activity. They wonder whether places could actually be haunted.

CHAPTER ONE

WHAT MAKES A HOUSE OR MANSION HAUNTED?

Most haunted houses and mansions have stories connected to them. These stories often involve death. For example, a murder might have taken place inside. Other stories might involve deaths from natural causes. Old houses and mansions may have a long history of different people living in it. And they often have reputations for being filled with ghosts.

Some supposedly haunted houses and mansions are abandoned while others are still lived in.

Ghosts are said to appear in many ways, including as mist, orbs, or full-bodied figures.

Some people think a person's spirit may haunt the place they died in. This can happen when the death was violent. A spirit may have an attachment to the house or mansion. It may not want to leave its home. Ghosts might also stay because they have unfinished business. This could be due to guilt. Or they did not get to do something while they lived.

Experts in the **paranormal** field describe signs that a house might be haunted. There could be a strange smell that cannot be explained. Another sign might be a sudden temperature drop in a section of a home. For example, a very cold spot may exist in the middle of a warm room. Out of the ordinary sounds could mean a place is haunted. This might be the sound of footsteps when only one person is home.

Haunted Houses Law

In 1989, Helen Ackley owned a supposedly haunted house. She eventually sold it to Jeffrey Stambovsky. Ackley did not tell Stambovsky that the house might be haunted. So he **sued** her. He won and got his money back. This case created a new law. It is illegal in some states to sell a house and not share that it could be haunted.

Or the sounds might come from objects moving on their own. These could all be signs of a haunting.

ARE GHOSTS REAL?

There is no solid proof that ghosts are real. But many people still believe in them. In a 2022 survey, 25 percent of US adults said they had lived in a haunted house. Scientists explain why people might have ghostly experiences. Some believe it is a person's brain playing tricks on them. A tired or worried person might imagine things. Seeing a ghost might be due to tricks of light.

Another possible explanation for seeing strange things is sleep **paralysis**. This happens just after a person falls asleep

Sleep paralysis can cause people to hallucinate, which means they see or hear things that are not actually there.

or wakes up. A person is awake. But they cannot move or speak. People with this condition often report seeing ghosts. They report hearing voices when no one else is there. Some people even describe feeling a dark force around them.

Adam Waytz is a **psychologist**. He thinks that people imagine things when their life feels out of control. Waytz says, "We create beliefs in ghosts, because we do not like believing that the universe is random."[1] People like to understand why certain things happen. The paranormal is one way to explain things that do not make sense.

HAUNTED HOUSES IN AMERICA

People have shared stories of haunted houses and mansions for centuries. There are more than 11,000 places in the United States that are said to be haunted. Many people have reported strange things happening in their home. They cannot explain what is happening. They wonder if their house might be haunted.

Several haunted houses and mansions in the United States are famous. One example

The LaLaurie Mansion is considered one of the most haunted houses in New Orleans, Louisiana.

is the White House. People have reported seeing ghosts there for hundreds of years. Some houses are said to have friendly ghosts. One of these is the Pittock Mansion in Portland, Oregon.

Some houses or mansions have grim stories. These homes may be the site of a crime. The John Sowden House is in Los Angeles, California. The house is known for its dark past. Another house with a tragic story is the Lizzie Borden House. It is in Fall River, Massachusetts. The house was the scene for two murders.

Other places are famous for being mysterious or strange. One of these is the Winchester Mystery House. It is in San Jose, California. The mansion was built by Sarah Winchester. Some people think she designed it to trick ghosts. Many people wonder whether these places are actually haunted.

The Sallie House in Atchison, Kansas, is believed to be haunted. Some visitors have reported being scratched and seeing objects move while there.

CHAPTER TWO

STORIES OF HAUNTED HOUSES AND MANSIONS

Haunted houses and mansions can be found around the world. One of the first haunted house stories was recorded around the first century CE. It was from a man named Pliny the Younger. He described a house in Athens, Greece. He said it was haunted by a ghost. The ghost had long hair and a beard. The ghost wore chains around its feet

In Pliny the Younger's story, a man named Athenodorus buys the haunted house and interacts with the ghost that lives there.

and hands. The chains rattled whenever the ghost moved.

Today, tales of haunted houses and mansions come from around the world. People can read these stories online or in books. Visiting one of these locations is often exciting and thrilling to people. Many wonder whether these stories could be true.

WHITE HOUSE GHOSTS

The White House is one of the most famous haunted mansions in the United States. It is located in Washington, DC. Past presidents and their wives reportedly haunt the rooms and hallways.

Thomas Jefferson was president from 1801 to 1809. Jefferson loved music. He often played the violin in the Yellow

Construction of the White House began in 1792.

Oval Room. After his death, other residents of the White House reported hearing violin music. It drifted down the hallways.

President Abraham Lincoln lived in the White House during the 1860s. His son Willie died there. Willie was 11 years old. Lincoln and his wife, Mary Todd Lincoln, reported seeing Willie's ghost. Mary claimed to see Willie's ghost at the foot of her bed. Some staff members also reported seeing

Willie's ghost. These reports came even after the Lincolns were no longer living in the White House.

The ghost of Lincoln is the most reported spirit in the White House. Many famous visitors have claimed to see him. One was British Prime Minister Winston Churchill.

President Abraham Lincoln's ghost has been reported in the Lincoln Bedroom and the Yellow Oval Room at the White House.

Churchill stayed in the White House in 1940. One night, he walked into his bedroom after taking a bath. He claimed he saw Lincoln's ghost standing by the fireplace. Churchill said to it, "Good evening, Mr. President. You seem to have me at a disadvantage."[2] The ghost then vanished. Churchill left the bedroom. He asked to never use it again.

PITTOCK MANSION GHOSTS

The Pittock Mansion is well known for its ghosts. It was designed by Henry Pittock. The forty-six-room mansion started being built in the early 1900s. It was finished in 1914. Pittock moved in with his wife, Georgina, and other family members. Four years later, Georgina died. Henry died a year after his wife.

The Pittock Mansion is an important part of Portland's history.

The Pittocks' relatives lived in the home until 1964. Then the city of Portland bought it. The city fixed it up. The mansion opened to the public in 1965. Some people claim that Henry and Georgina still haunt the mansion. They believe the couple want visitors to feel welcome in their home.

People have had strange experiences in the mansion. Some say they smell roses throughout the house. Roses were Georgina's favorite flower.

Tour guides have also reported seeing figures in the mansion. Spirits are said to move furniture and house plants around in the rooms. A woman in a long gown was once spotted picking up a picture off the ground. The woman quickly vanished. Another time a staff member turned off all the lights for the night. She locked up the mansion. She began to walk away. Then she saw all the lights in the mansion switch back on.

Visitors to the house have reported seeing other strange things. Windows are said to shut and lock on their own.

Some people hear the sound of footsteps. Others have even claimed to see the ghostly figures of the Pittocks.

HOBO HILL HOUSE

Aaron and Erin Clark bought a historic home in 2017. It was called the Hobo Hill House. The house is in Jefferson City, Missouri. It was named after an area in the city.

The house was built in 1910. It needed to be fixed up. The Clarks hired workers to do the job. Some workers reported feeling as though they were punched. But when they turned around, they did not see anyone.

The Clarks moved in once the house was ready. They also noticed strange

Some people claim that restoring an old house can disturb the spirits that live there.

things there. The lights, television, and space heaters turned on by themselves. The Clarks heard sounds such as loud bangs and creaks. Items moved around the house. The family dog would not go near certain areas of the house. It avoided the stairs, attic, and basement.

The couple said they often saw a tall man in a suit and top hat. He would be in the corner of a room. Their daughter claimed to hear a voice. It said, "Hi." The Clarks did not feel safe in their home. Erin said, "It was the scariest thing I ever experienced because it was the fear of the unknown."[3]

The Clarks decided to investigate further. They spoke with people who had previously lived there. Almost everyone reported the same ghostly experiences. The couple heard reports that the house had once held prisoners. They remembered seeing cell-like cages in the basement before the house was worked on.

The couple lived in the Hobo Hill House for only 7 months. They decided it was too spooky to live there. The house was then turned into a short-term rental property. Many guests wanted to spend a few nights in the supposedly haunted house.

People are curious about the paranormal. Some decide to investigate claims of hauntings. They want to help others understand unexplained events.

Unexpected Roommate

Some spirits are said to be friendly. Brandy Fleischer lived in a house built in the 1800s. The house is in Genoa City, Wisconsin. Fleischer believed she shared her home with a ghost. She called him Henry. Fleischer said, "He likes to play pranks. He'll move shoes around." She said living with Henry was like having a roommate.

Quoted in Anna Kodé, "How to Live With a Ghost," New York Times, *October 26, 2022. www.nytimes.com.*

CHAPTER THREE

GHOST HUNTERS

Experts in ghost hunting are called paranormal investigators. They gather evidence in places that might be haunted. They look at that evidence to determine whether a house or mansion is haunted. Some of the tools they use include video cameras and voice recorders.

Ghost hunters travel to supposedly haunted places around the world. But they may not find any evidence of ghosts.

Many ghost hunters research a place before they investigate it to learn more about its history.

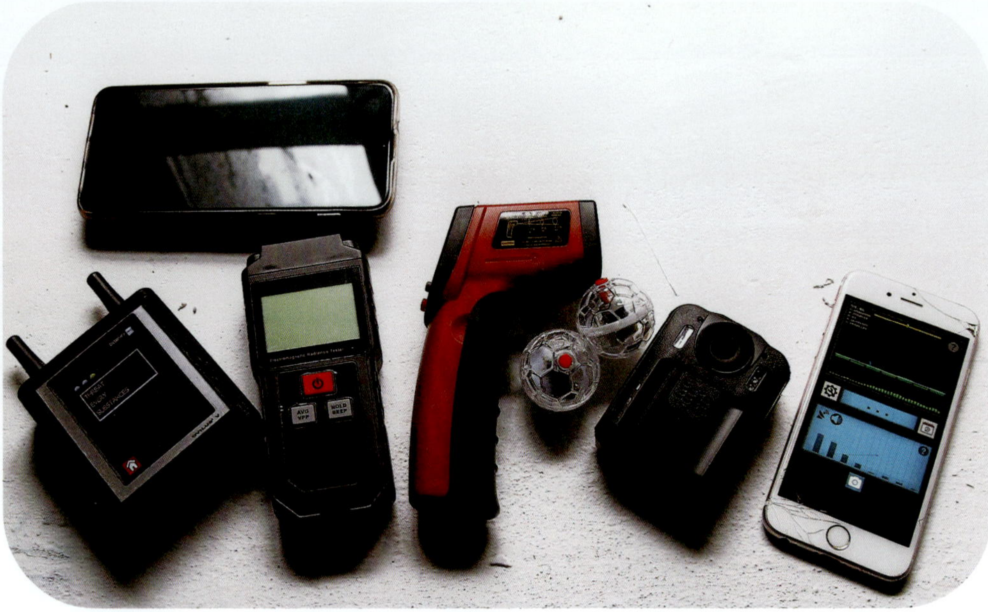

Paranormal investigators use a variety of equipment to search for evidence of ghosts.

Laura Pennace is a paranormal investigator. She believes the first step is to try to find a scientific explanation for what is going on. She says, “It is important not to jump to the idea that anything is a ghost.”[4]

THE AMITYVILLE HORROR HOUSE

Ed and Lorraine Warren were paranormal investigators. The couple was called to investigate a famous case at a house in

Amityville, New York. The house was known as the Amityville Horror House. A man named Ronald DeFeo Jr. killed his family there in 1974.

Two years later, the Lutz family moved in. But they left after just 28 days. The family claimed to see slime oozing out of the walls. They said knives would fly off the counters. At night, they claimed they would float above their beds. The family believed a ghost was living in the house. They hired the Warrens to investigate.

The Warrens reported being pushed to the floor. They claimed to have taken a picture of a spirit in the home's basement. It looked like a child. The Warrens looked into the history of the house. They learned that American Indians had once owned the land the house was built on. Bodies had been buried there. The Warrens decided the Amityville property might also be haunted by the spirits of those buried.

However, many people did not believe the house was haunted. In 2000, a reporter from the newspaper *The Amityville Record*

Several movies based on the haunted history of the Amityville Horror House have come out since 1979.

visited the house. It had new owners. The owners said nothing strange ever happened to them. The newspaper reported, "It is just another house in Amityville with nothing more than a horrific history."[5]

THE JOHN SOWDEN HOUSE

Steve Gonsalves is a paranormal investigator. He often appeared on a TV series. It is called *Ghost Hunters*. Gonsalves founded The Atlantic Paranormal Society, or TAPS. One of Gonsalves's most memorable cases was at the John Sowden House in Los Angeles.

George Hodel once owned the home. He lived there in 1945. Hodel was a suspect in the murders of several women. But he was never charged with any crimes. After Hodel

The John Sowden House was built in 1926. It was named after John Sowden, for whom the house was built.

died, many people lived in the house. Some people reported hearing strange voices. They claimed to hear dragging sounds in the hallways. Others reported seeing female ghosts in the basement.

During his investigation, Gonsalves heard footsteps close behind him. When he turned around, he did not see anyone.

He also heard sounds of things being pulled off a table. Gonsalves also recorded several voices during the investigation. One sounded like a child. Another sounded like a woman struggling.

Gonsalves felt a darkness in the John Sowden House. He said, "I felt that darkness cling to me for weeks following the investigation."[6] This is why many ghost hunters continue searching for paranormal evidence there.

HOUSE CALLS

The Paranormal Investigators of Milwaukee make house calls to supposedly haunted places. The group looks for evidence of ghosts. Michael Graeve and Randy Soukup were two investigators in the group.

In one case, Graeve and Soukup visited a home. It was rented by José, Maria, and their five daughters. Their 10-year-old daughter Jasmine reported seeing the ghost of a little girl. The ghost was dressed in a dirty, white dress. She had black hair that hung over her face. Another daughter said the ghost pulled her hair. It also sat at the foot of her bed and in her closet.

The ghost hunters walked through the house. They wanted to see if there was a simple explanation for what might be happening. Soukup swept the room with his electromagnetic field (EMF) meter. But he did not seem to find anything.

Graeve asked José whether Jasmine watched a lot of scary movies. He thought Jasmine's ghost sounded similar to one from a movie. Movies and stories about ghosts can sometimes fuel people's imaginations. Graeve said, "The whole family feeds off each other's stories, which makes tricks of the mind easier."[7]

There is no proof that ghosts exist. But many people still believe that hauntings are real. They continue to investigate supposedly haunted houses and mansions.

EMF Meters

EMF meters are a common piece of ghost hunting equipment. They detect electromagnetic fields. These are areas with electrical and magnetic energy. Many people think ghosts release large amounts of energy. EMF meters can pick up areas in homes where more energy is present. Ghost hunters use EMF meters to find evidence of ghosts.

TOURS AND EXPERIENCES

People have been fascinated with tales of haunted houses and mansions for centuries. In 1915, a British man named Patrick Collins built a fake haunted house. He sold tickets to visitors. He called his attraction the Orton and Spooner Ghost House. It was the first recorded haunted house built as a money-making, thrill experience.

Some supposedly haunted houses and mansions have been turned into museums, such as the Whaley House in San Diego, California.

THE
WHALEY
HOUSE
MUSEUM
AMERICA'S MOST HAUNTED HOUSE.

Some people travel long distances to visit spooky houses and mansions. They take tours through them. Some people will even spend the night in one. Today, there are more than 1,200 haunted attractions in the United States. People pay to visit them. Visiting haunted homes is especially popular around Halloween.

Disney's Haunted Mansion

In 1961, Walt Disney built a haunted mansion in his Disneyland theme park in California. It was an instant success. The ride was designed to scare people. Monsters popped out from behind headstones. Ghosts moved around, spoke, and sang. Disney inspired other companies to offer spooky experiences to visitors.

THE WINCHESTER MYSTERY HOUSE

The Winchester Mystery House is in San Jose. It is famous for its ghostly sightings and strange **architecture**. The mansion was built by Sarah Winchester.

Sarah was married to a man named William Winchester. His family made and

The Winchester Mystery house is 24,000 square feet (2,230 sq m) and has 160 rooms.

sold guns. They were called Winchester rifles. Sarah believed that the spirits of the people killed by these rifles were haunting her. She wanted to live in her mansion in peace. So she designed it to confuse the ghosts she thought were haunting her.

The mansion opened to the public after Sarah died in 1922. Janan Boehme is an expert on the house's history. Boehme said that tourists come visit to see the strange, spooky house. The daily mansion tour is the most popular attraction. Visitors climb staircases that lead to nowhere. They also search for openings in walls to find hidden passageways.

Many different tours have been offered at the mansion. One was the Flashlight Tour. On this tour, visitors explored the mansion

The grand ballroom, parlor, and basement are some of the many rooms in the Winchester Mystery House where people report paranormal activity.

after dark. They also heard stories about people who once lived there. Visitors could visit the **séance** room as well. Sarah held séances every night.

During Halloween, the mansion would become even spookier. Actors played the roles of the ghosts. One Halloween tour was called Unhinged. It featured a light show. The show highlighted the unique parts of the house. A ghostly **silhouette** would sometimes show up on a wall. There was also an indoor maze. The maze went through three floors of the house.

LIZZIE BORDEN HOUSE

The Lizzie Borden House is located in Massachusetts. It is the site of two unsolved murders. In 1892, Lizzie Borden was accused of killing her father and stepmother. She is believed to have killed them with an ax in their home. But Borden was not charged with the murders. The crime was never solved. Over the years, people never forgot this murder mystery.

The company US Ghost Adventures now owns the Lizzie Borden House. Many people come to visit it every year.

Some visitors to the Lizzie Borden House have claimed to take photos with unexplained faces in them.

Guests can tour the house. Some people have reported having their ears pulled. Others have claimed to see figures moving in the rooms. A ghostly woman is often

Many ghost tours have guides who talk about the history of a supposedly haunted location. Guides might also share the ghostly experiences reported there.

seen in her nightgown. Some believe she is the ghost of Borden's stepmother.

Visitors can also stay overnight in the house. Erika Mailman was one visitor who stayed there. Mailman was scared to sleep in the house. She said, "It was creepy to be in the house. . . . Knowing that two people had met their [**demise**] in such a violent way was definitely disturbing."[8]

That was also part of the reason Mailman wanted to stay there. She left her bedside lamp on all night. She did not experience any paranormal activity. But she did have a nightmare about a little girl trapped in a closet.

Visitors of the Lizzie Borden House can also go on haunted walking tours. They can tour Oak Grove Cemetery. Borden and her family are buried there. The cemetery is 1.5 miles (2.4 km) from the house.

Many guests also take part in a nighttime ghost hunt. People get their own ghost hunting equipment. They try to solve the mystery of what happened on the day of the murders. One group investigates the first floor. It is where one body was found.

Experts say that a person's brain can sometimes play tricks on them and make them think they see a ghost.

Although there is no proof that ghosts exist, that does not stop people from investigating supposedly haunted houses and mansions.

The other group investigates the basement. It looks for ghosts and clues.

CONTINUING THE SEARCH

People continue to be fascinated by haunted houses and mansions. Ghost hunters investigate to try to find evidence of spirits. They search for proof that a

FAMOUS HAUNTED HOUSES AND MANSIONS IN THE UNITED STATES

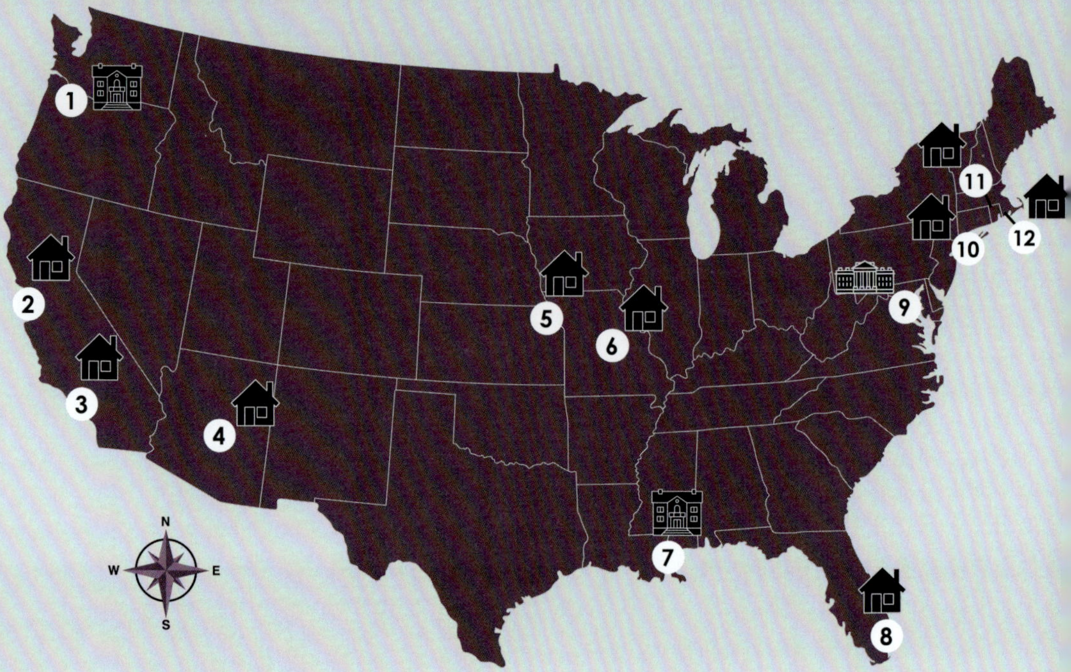

1. Pittock Mansion:
Portland, Oregon

2. Winchester Mystery House:
San Jose, California

3. John Sowden House:
Los Angeles, California

4. Rosson House:
Phoenix, Arizona

5. Sallie House:
Atchison, Kansas

6. Hobo Hill House:
Jefferson City, Missouri

7. LaLaurie Mansion:
New Orleans, Louisiana

8. Stranahan House:
Fort Lauderdale, Florida

9. The White House:
Washington, DC

10. Amityville Horror House:
Amityville, New York

11. Conjuring House:
Burrillville, Rhode Island

12. Lizzie Borden House:
Fall River, Massachusetts

Many houses and mansions across the United States are believed to be haunted.

house is haunted. Today, many supposedly haunted houses and mansions are open for public tours or overnight stays. People go in the hopes of witnessing something paranormal.

Colin Dickey is the author of the book *Ghostland: An American History in Haunted Places*. Dickey says, "A home is a place that is supposed to feel safe and warm and comforting."[9] He believes haunted houses challenge people's ideas of being in a safe place. That is why so many find these locations to be scary.

GLOSSARY

architecture

the design or style of a building

demise

death

paralysis

a state in which a person or thing cannot move

paranormal

something that is unexplained by science, such as ghosts or aliens

psychologist

a specialist who studies mind and behavior or one who diagnoses and treats mental health conditions

séance

a ritual where people try to connect with the dead

silhouette

the dark outline of a body against something lighter

sued

brought legal action against a person or organization

SOURCE NOTES

CHAPTER ONE: WHAT MAKES A HOUSE OR MANSION HAUNTED?

1. Quoted in David Robson, "Psychology: The Truth About the Paranormal," *BBC*, October 30, 2024. www.bbc.com.

CHAPTER TWO: STORIES OF HAUNTED HOUSES AND MANSIONS

2. Quoted in Katherine Brodt, "The Legends of Lincoln's Ghost," *Boundary Stones,* October 29, 2020. https://boundarystones.weta.org.

3. Quoted in "A Family's American Dream Home Turned Horror Story," *Jefferson City Magazine*, n.d. https://jeffersoncitymag.com.

CHAPTER THREE: GHOST HUNTERS

4. Quoted in Candace Braun Davison and Hadley Mendelsohn, "5 Signs Your House Might Be Haunted," *House Beautiful*, July 10, 2023. www.housebeautiful.com.

5. Quoted in Gavin Newsham, "'Amityville Horror' 50 Years Later—A Look at the 'Most Haunted House in the World' Decades After Grisly Killings," *New York Post*, November 9, 2024. https://nypost.com.

6. Steve Gonsalves, *A Life with Ghosts*. Gallery Books, 2023, pp. 212–213.

7. Tea Krulos, *Monster Hunters*. Chicago Review Press, 2015, p. 90.

CHAPTER FOUR: TOURS AND EXPERIENCES

8. Quoted in Erika Mailman, "I Spent the Night in the Lizzie Borden Murder House and It Was Legit Creepy," *TimeOut*, October 31, 2022. www.timeout.com.

9. Quoted in Sophie Caldwell, "10 Haunted Houses to Visit During Spooky Season," *Today*, October 31, 2024. www.today.com.

FOR FURTHER RESEARCH

BOOKS

Carla Mooney, *Hauntings*. BrightPoint Press, 2025.

Tim Rayborn, *The Big Book of Paranormal: 300 Mystical and Frightening Tales from Around the World*. Applesauce Press, 2021.

Thomas Kingsley Troupe, *Haunted Houses and Mansions*. Crabtree Publishing Company, 2022.

INTERNET SOURCES

"How to Hunt Ghosts," *Ghosts and Gravestones*, n.d. www.ghostsandgravestones.com.

Janet Loehrke, "Is the White House Haunted? Spooky Stories Reveal a History of the Supernatural," *USA Today*, October 26, 2024. www.usatoday.com.

"The Spooktacular History of the Haunted House," *BBC*, October 13, 2023. www.bbc.co.uk.

WEBSITES

Boston Ghosts

https://bostonghosts.com

Boston Ghosts is a tour company that takes guests to places around the Boston, Massachusetts, area that are thought to be haunted. The site has a blog with information about supposedly haunted houses and mansions near the city, including the Perron farmhouse.

US Ghost Adventures

https://usghostadventures.com

US Ghost Adventures provides tours across the country at places believed to be haunted. The website features a blog where people can learn about the haunted history of different locations.

Winchester Mystery House

https://winchestermysteryhouse.com

This website describes the different tours and what visitors can explore at the Winchester Mystery House. The site has historic photographs and more information about Sarah Winchester and her house.

INDEX

IMAGE CREDITS

Cover: © Muhammad Tauseef Tauseef/Shutterstock Images
5: © Heidi Schneider/Shutterstock Images
7: © Katyplace/Shutterstock Images
8: © Zef Art/Shutterstock Images
9: © Sergey Nivens/Shutterstock Images
10: © mRGB/Shutterstock Images
13: © As Above Media/Shutterstock Images
14: © Zef Art/Shutterstock Images
17: © Uvgreen/Shutterstock Images
19: © JustPixs/Shutterstock Images
21: © DonsESLAdventure/iStockphoto
23: © Chronicle/Alamy
25: © Orhan Cam/Shutterstock Images
26: © Anthony Berger/Library of Congress
28: © Carol M. Highsmith/Library of Congress
31: © Vladimir Mulder/Shutterstock Images
35: © Marijan Murat/picture-alliance/dpa/AP Images
36: © Sean Aidan Calderbank/Shutterstock Images
38: © John Arehart/Shutterstock Images
40: © MSPhotographic/Shutterstock Images
45: © RoamingPanda/iStockphoto
47: © JHVEPhoto/Shutterstock Images
49: © DreamArt123/Shutterstock Images
51: © Jim McIntosh/Flickr
52: © Heidi Besen/Shutterstock Images
54: © Zef Art/Shutterstock Images
55: © Jeffrey Legitt/Shutterstock Images
56 (houses): © phipatbig/Shutterstock Images
56 (mansions): © microicon/Shutterstock Images
56 (map, White House): © Red Line Editorial

ABOUT THE AUTHOR

Janie Havemeyer is the author of many books for young readers. She lives in San Francisco, California. Every Halloween, her neighborhood is filled with elaborate haunted house displays and spooky decorations.